ICONS

TAYLOR SWIFT

BY BETH GOTTLIEB

Enslow PUBLISHING

Please visit our website, www.enslow.com.
For a free color catalog of all our high-quality books, call toll free 1-800-398-2504 or fax 1-877-980-4454.

Library of Congress Cataloging-in-Publication Data
Names: Gottlieb, Beth, author.
Title: Taylor Swift / Beth Gottlieb.
Description: Buffalo, NY : Enslow Publishing, 2025. | Series: Icons | Includes index.
Identifiers: LCCN 2023053112 | ISBN 9781978540224 (library binding) | ISBN 9781978540217 (paperback) | ISBN 9781978540231 (ebook)
Subjects: LCSH: Swift, Taylor, 1989---Juvenile literature. | Singers--United States--Biography--Juvenile literature. | Country musicians--United States--Biography--Juvenile literature.
Classification: LCC ML3930.S989 G67 2025 | DDC 782.421642092 [B]--dc23/eng/20231114
LC record available at https://lccn.loc.gov/2023053112

Published in 2025 by
Enslow Publishing
2544 Clinton Street
Buffalo, NY 14224

Designer: Tanya Dellaccio Keeney
Editor: Kristen Rajczak Nelson

Photo credits: Cover Cover AFF/Alamy.com; pp. 5, 29 MediaPunch Inc/Alamy.com; p. 7 s_bukley/Shutterstock.com; p. 9 Everett Collection/Shutterstock.com; p. 11 Debby Wong/Shutterstock.com; pp. 13, 15 Featureflash Photo Agency/Shutterstock.com; p. 17 Ovidiu Hrubaru/Shutterstock.com; p. 18 Michael R Helland/Shutterstock.com; pp. 19, 21, 23 Tinseltown/Shutterstock.com; p. 20 hakanyalicn/Shutterstock.com; pp 22,24 melissamn/Shutterstock.com; p. 25 PA Images/Alamy.com; pp. 26, 27 Paolo Villanueva/Flickr.com.

Printed in the United States of America

CPSIA compliance information: Batch #CSENS25: For further information contact Enslow Publishing, at 1-800-398-2504.

Contents

Words in the glossary appear in **bold** the first time they are used in the text.

Fearless Taylor

Taylor Swift has sold millions of albums and played sold out concerts all over the world. She has **reinvented** herself more than once, gaining fans each time. Through it all, Taylor has stayed connected to her Swifties, or loyal fans. She is an **icon**!

ICONIC!

Taylor told Time *magazine in 2014: "The challenge with a* ***stadium*** *show is making those people in the very top row feel like they got an intimate, personal experience."*

Young Artist

Taylor was born in Pennsylvania in 1989. She liked singing and writing. Taylor recorded music for the first time at age 11. She tried to get a record deal too! A few years later, her family moved near Nashville, Tennessee, to support her dreams of being a musician.

ICONIC!

In 2005, Taylor signed a deal with Big Machine Records. She was just 15!

Taylor's first album, *Taylor Swift*, was a country album. It sold 500,000 copies in its first three months it was out! *Fearless* came out in 2008 and won Taylor a Grammy Award for Album of the Year. At that point, she was the youngest person ever to win that award.

ICONIC!

As of 2024, Taylor has won 14 Grammy Awards including three more for Album of the Year.

GRAMMY AWARDS
AWARDS
AWARDS

Finding Her Voice

Taylor had written some of the songs on her first two albums. The others she co-wrote. But when her third album *Speak Now* came out in 2010, it had 14 songs on it—all written by Taylor alone.

ICONIC!

Taylor draws from her own life when writing songs. It has made fans try to figure out who or what certain songs are about!

Taylor's sound started to change with *Red*, which came out in 2012. Her songs started to sound more like pop. "We Are Never Ever Getting Back Together" was a hit for pop and country fans. It was Taylor's first No. 1 song on the *Billboard* Hot 100!

ICONIC!

Taylor won the Country Music Award for Entertainer of the Year after Red *came out. She won the award in 2009 too, making her the youngest person to ever win it.*

GRAMMY
GRAMMY AWARDS
GRAMMY
GRAMMY

Making a Change

In 2013, Taylor moved from outside Nashville to New York City. By this time, everything Taylor did was news. She was **criticized** a lot, including about who her friends were and what she wore. So Taylor did what she does best: she wrote songs about what she was going through.

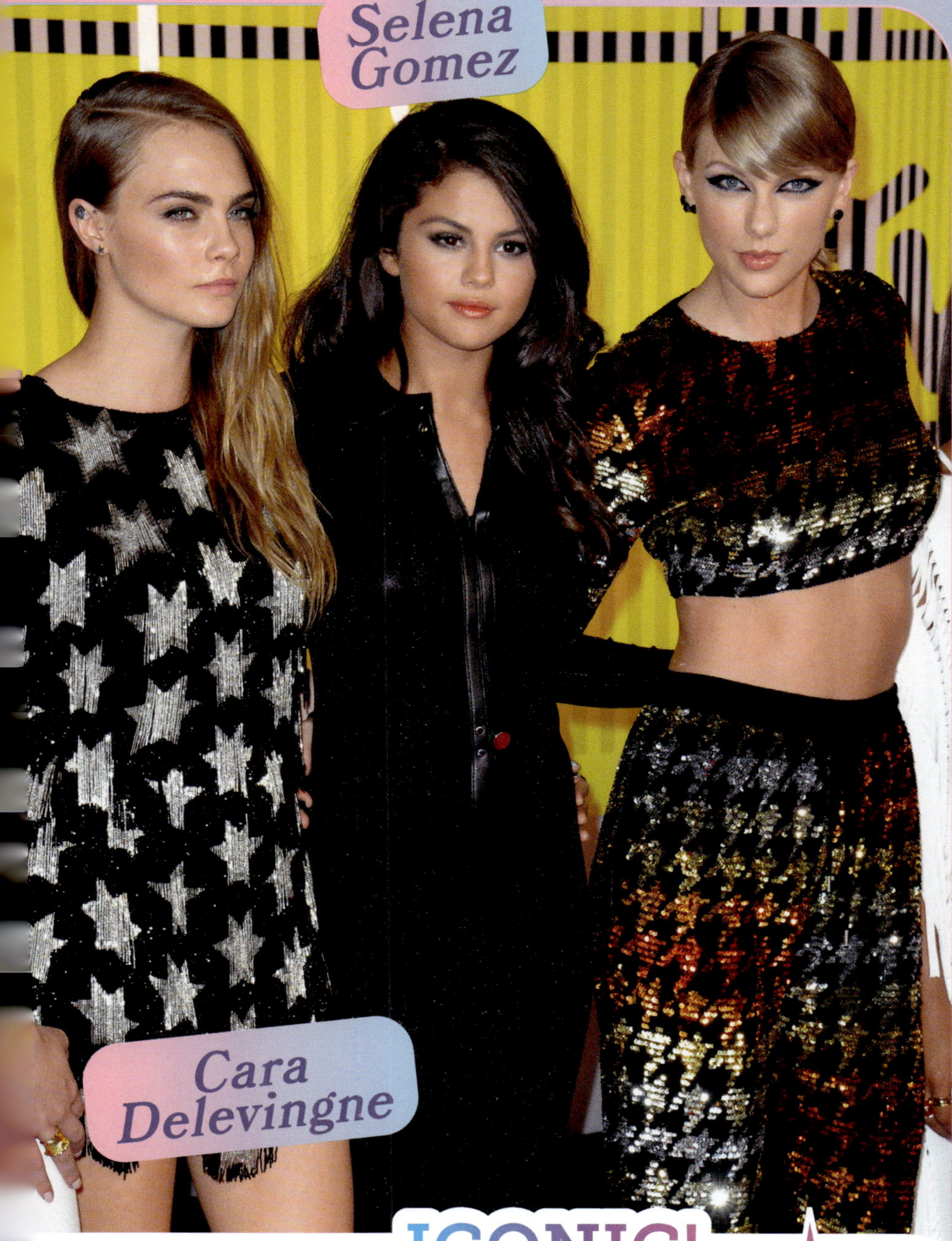

ICONIC!

Taylor has appeared in a few movies, including The Giver *in 2014 and* Cats *in 2019.*

Taylor's album *1989* came out in 2014 to huge sales. It sold more than 1 million copies in its first week! Hit songs from 1989, including "Shake It Off" and "Bad Blood," showed that Taylor had fully crossed over into pop music.

ICONIC!

Since 2014, 1989 *has gone platinum nine times. Platinum means an album or song has sold 1 million copies. Musicians are given a special record when this happens!*

The Price of Fame

Taylor's life continued to make headlines. The hip-hop pop sound of *Reputation*, which came out in 2017, included songs about how hard being in the spotlight could be. Taylor wrote some songs from the **point of view** of another character, not herself.

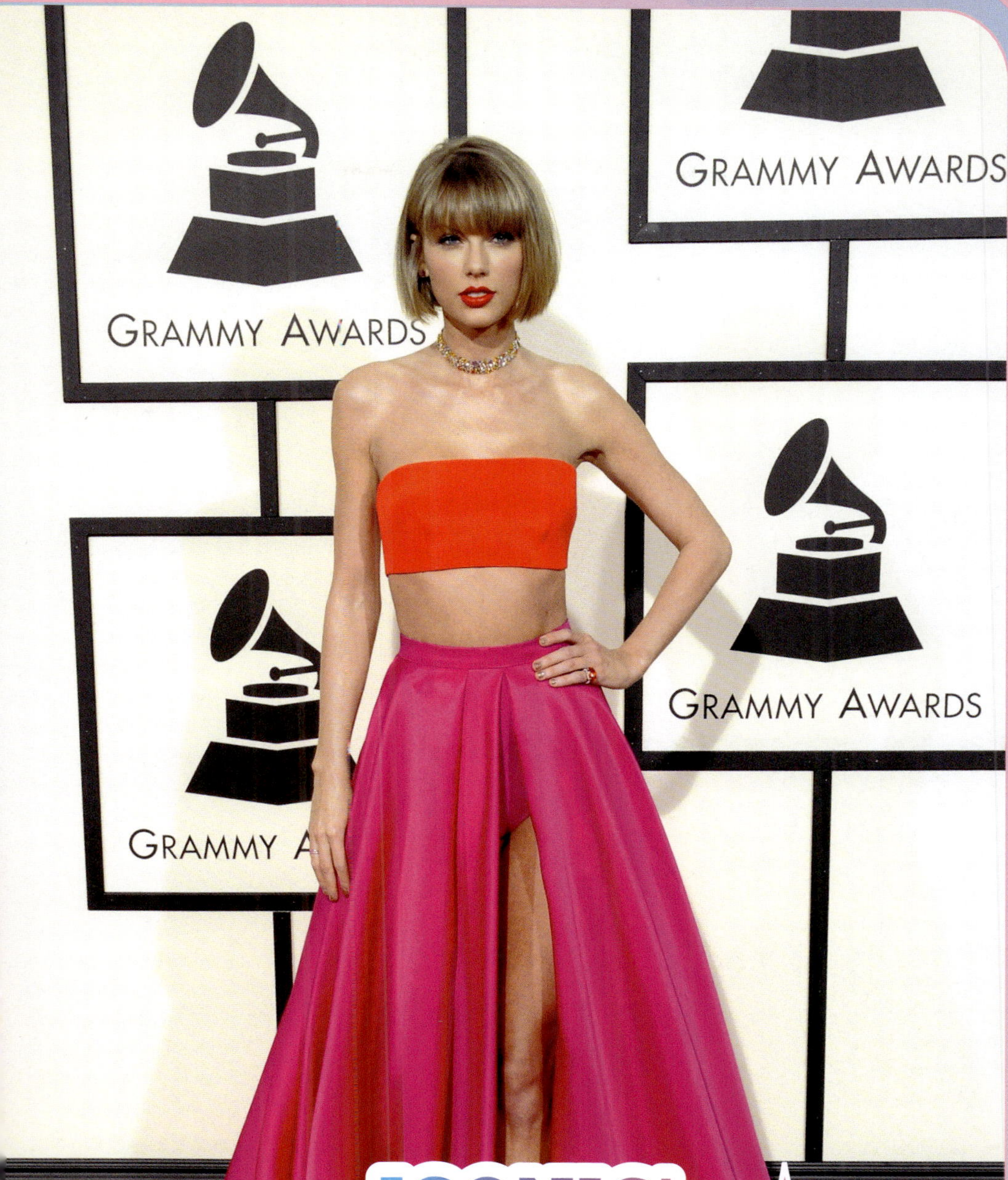

ICONIC!

Taylor has used her fame to speak out about what she thinks is important. She has told young people to vote, spoken in favor of laws, and supported LGBTQ+ rights.

Begin Again

Taylor went on **tour** for *Reputation* in 2018. Soon after, she left Big Machine Records. The label went on to sell her **master recordings**. Taylor was angry—but she decided to move on and keep making music for her fans.

ICONIC!

Taylor put out the album Lover *in 2019 on a new record label. She told* Vogue *at the time: "There are so many ways in which this album feels like a new beginning."*

Taylor put out two albums in 2020: *folklore* and *evermore*. Taylor showed yet another change in her sound on these albums. The songs of both albums were quieter and more thoughtful—and fans loved them! *Folklore* won the Grammy Award for Album of the Year.

ICONIC!

Since Taylor didn't own the masters of her first albums, she decided to re-record them! By 2023, Taylor's ***versions*** *of* Fearless, Red, Speak Now, *and* 1989 *had come out.*

Setting Records

Midnights came out at midnight on October 21, 2022. It set world records, including being the most-streamed album ever in 24 hours on Spotify. More than 184 million people streamed it to set that record!

ICONIC!

Taylor has directed many of her own music videos! She also wrote and directed All Too Well: The Short Film, *which came out in 2021.*

The Eras Tour

Taylor set out on her biggest tour yet in March 2023. Each show on The Eras Tour was three or more hours, showcasing songs from all the albums Taylor had made so far. The tour was the highest grossing, or most money-making, tour ever!

ICONIC!

Taylor Swift: The Eras Tour *movie has made the most money of any concert movie ever!*

Truly Taylor

Taylor won Album of the Year for the fourth time at the 2024 Grammy Awards, in addition to another Grammy! She also put out another album: *The Tortured Poets Department.* No matter the ups and downs of her time in the spotlight, Taylor is truly an icon!

ICONIC!

*Taylor has remained a **role model** for many fans. She works hard, stands up for herself, and is always growing and changing.*

Taylor's Music Timeline

2005 *Taylor signs with Big Machine Records in Nashville.*

2006 *Her first album,* Taylor Swift, *comes out.*

2008 Fearless *comes out.*

2010 Speak Now *comes out.*

2012 Red *comes out.*

2014 *Taylor puts out* 1989, *her first totally pop album.*

2017 Reputation *comes out.*

2018 *Taylor leaves Big Machine Records.*

2019 *She puts out* Lover *on a new label.*

2020 Folklore *and* evermore *come out.*

2021 *Taylor's versions of* Fearless *and* Red *come out.*

2022 Midnights *comes out, breaking streaming records.*

2023 *Taylor starts The Eras Tour. Her versions of* Speak Now *and* 1989 *come out.*

2024 The Tortured Poets Department *comes out.*

For More Information

BOOKS

Daniels, Rachel. *Meet Taylor Swift!* Hallandale, FL: Mitchell Lane Publishers, 2024.

Marx, Grace Rapone. *What You Never Knew About Taylor Swift.* North Mankato, MN: Capstone Press, 2023.

Rose, Rachel. *Taylor Swift: Singer, Songwriter, and Activist.* Minneapolis, MN: Bearport Publishing Company, 2023.

WEBSITE

Taylor Swift's Official Website

www.taylorswift.com/

Keep up with Taylor's latest music and tour information on her official website.

Publisher's note to educators and parents: Our editors have carefully reviewed these websites to ensure that they are suitable for students. Many websites change frequently, however, and we cannot guarantee that a site's future contents will continue to meet our high standards of quality and educational value. Be advised that students should be closely supervised whenever they access the internet.

Glossary

criticize: To talk about someone's problems or faults, or to express disapproval of someone or something.

icon: A person who is very successful and admired.

master recording: The official, original recording of a song. They are sometimes just called masters.

point of view: A way of looking at or thinking about something.

reinvent: To make big changes, often to make something better.

role model: Someone who other people look up to and try to be like.

stadium: A large, sometimes roofless, building with a large open area and many seats commonly used for sports events and concerts.

tour: A trip to many places in order to play and sing music for people.

version: A form of something that is different from others.

Index